M000286392

the good life

BIBLE STUDY

LifeWay Press®
Nashville, Tennessee

Editorial Team

Scott Latta
Content Editor

Morgan Hawk
Production Editor

Amy Lyon
Graphic Designer

Karen Daniel
Editorial Team Leader

John Paul Basham
Manager, Student Ministry Publishing

Ben Trueblood
Director, Student Ministry

Published by LifeWay Press® • © 2020 Derwin L. Gray

No part of this book may be reproduced or transmitted in any form or by any means, electronic or mechanical, including photocopying and recording, or by any information storage or retrieval system, except as may be expressly permitted in writing by the publisher. Requests for permission should be addressed in writing to LifeWay Press®; One LifeWay Plaza; Nashville, TN 37234.

ISBN 978-1-0877-2437-9 • Item 005828211

Dewey decimal classification: 248.84

Subject headings: CHRISTIAN LIFE / HAPPINESS / BEATITUDES

All Scripture quotations are taken from the Christian Standard Bible®, Copyright © 2017 by Holman Bible Publishers. Used by permission. Christian Standard Bible® and CSB® are federally registered trademarks of Holman Bible Publishers.

To order additional copies of this resource, write to LifeWay Resources Customer Service; One LifeWay Plaza; Nashville, TN 37234; fax 615-251-5933; call toll free 800-458-2772; order online at LifeWay.com; or email orderentry@lifeway.com.

Printed in the United States of America.

Student Ministry Publishing • LifeWay Resources • One LifeWay Plaza • Nashville, TN 37234

Contents

About the Author

Dr. Derwin L. Gray is the founding and lead pastor of Transformation Church, a multiethnic, multigenerational, mission-shaped community just south of Charlotte, North Carolina. After graduating from Brigham Young University, Derwin played professional football in the NFL for five years with the Indianapolis Colts (1993-1997) and one year with the Carolina Panthers (1998). During that time, he and his wife, Vicki, began their journey with Christ and experienced God's faithfulness and direction as He moved their hearts to know Him and make Him known. In addition to his role at Transformation Church, Derwin speaks at conferences nationwide. He is the author of *Hero: Unleashing God's Power in a Man's Heart* (2010), *Limitless Life: You Are More Than Your Past When God Holds Your Future* (2013), *Crazy Grace for Crazy Times* (2015), and *The High-Definition Leader* (2015).

the good life . . .

that we desire and, more importantly, were created for is available to us.

Two thousand years ago, on a hill overlooking the Sea of Galilee, our good King invited us to discover the happiness we long to experience. The invitation still stands. You don't have to chase shadows anymore. Jesus—happiness himself—is chasing you.

are you ready?

HOW TO USE THIS STUDY

Group Sessions

Regardless of what day of the week your group meets, each week of content begins with the group session. Each group session uses the following format to facilitate simple yet meaningful interaction among group members with God's Word and with the video teaching from Pastor Derwin.

START. This page includes questions to get the conversation started and to introduce the video teaching.

WATCH. This page provides space to take notes on the video teaching.

DISCUSS. This page includes questions and statements that guide the group to respond to Pastor Derwin's teaching and explore relevant Bible passages.

Personal Study

Each week provides three days of Bible study and learning activities for individual engagement between group sessions. The personal study revisits stories, Scriptures, and themes introduced in the video teaching so participants can understand and apply them on a personal level.

Each personal study includes the following three sections.[1]

UPWARD. Loving God completely is a growth process that involves the personal elements of communication and response. By listening to the Holy Spirit in the words of Scripture and speaking to the Lord in our thoughts and prayers, we move in the direction of knowing Him better. The better we know Him, the more we'll love Him, and the more we love Him, the greater will be our willingness to respond to Him in trust and obedience.

INWARD. To love ourselves correctly is to see ourselves as God sees us and to allow the Word, not the world, to define who and whose we really are. The clearer we capture the vision of our new identity in Jesus Christ, the more we'll realize that our deepest needs for security, significance, and satisfaction are met in Him and not in people, possessions, or positions.

OUTWARD. A biblical view of our identity and resources in Christ moves us in the direction of loving others compassionately. Grasping our true and unlimited resources in Christ frees us from bondage to the opinions of others and gives us the liberty to love and serve others regardless of their responses.

1. Upward, Inward, Outward originated in the work of theologian Ken Boa. See Ken Boa, *Face to Face: Praying the Scriptures for Intimate Worship* (Grand Rapids, Zondervan, 1997).

Week 1
the good life

HAPPY ARE THE
Beggars

WELCOME TO SESSION 1

**Would you say most people you know
are happy? Why or why not?**

What are some ways people seek to achieve happiness?

We're all hardwired to search for happiness, but at some point in our lives, we realize no matter how hard and how long we work, we'll never achieve lasting happiness. The kind of happiness we long for isn't about perpetually feeling good or good things consistently happening to us. The happiness we're hardwired for can only be found in Jesus.

Over the next eight weeks, I'll lead us through the Beatitudes and help us learn how to experience the good life.

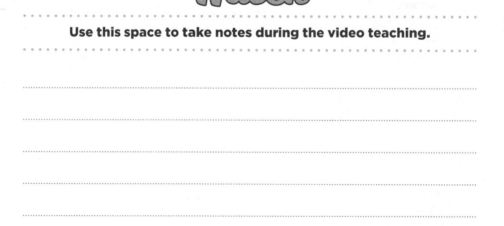

Use this space to take notes during the video teaching.

Discuss

Read Jesus' words together.

Blessed are the poor in spirit,
for the kingdom of heaven is theirs.
MATTHEW 5:3

How has this week's teaching changed your understanding of what it means to be "poor in spirit"?

Why is becoming poor in spirit so unnatural for us?

When did you first realize your spiritual poverty? How has your life changed since that moment?

Pride blinds us to our need for grace. When has your pride blinded you to God's grace?

How is God extending grace to you right now? How does reflecting upon that grace make you feel toward God?

True happiness comes from becoming more like Jesus. Jesus fully depended upon God. How can you depend more on God and less on yourself over the next week?

OVER THE NEXT WEEK
Marinate on This

Being poor in spirit means we're humble enough to receive the unsearchable riches of Christ.

Being poor in spirit means you see and accept your spiritual bankruptcy so you can make room for Christ's treasures.

We were created to be completely confident and reliant on God. It's only in our weakness that God shares His strength with us.

We can't be poor in spirit when we're seeking to rule ourselves. We can't live the good life when we're wrapped up in our sinfulness.

We can look to Jesus as the ultimate example of happiness because happiness is found in becoming a person who projects the character of Jesus into the world.

The happiness of God's kingdom isn't about perpetually feeling good; it's about the happiness expressed in the Beatitudes, which helps us become like Christ.

Jesus' circumstances were the window through which He expressed His happiness—they weren't the cause of his happiness. Our circumstances do not add or take away from our happiness.

The deeper we immerse ourselves in Jesus and His kingdom, the more He sculpts us into His image and the happier we become.

Blessed are the
POOR IN SPIRIT,
for the kingdom of heaven is theirs.

MATTHEW 5:3

LIFE, LIBERTY, AND HAPPINESS

How have you tried to find happiness?

Growing up in the United States, you learn from an early age that the good life—the right to be happy—is a fundamental right. The pursuit of happiness is written into the DNA of this country. Way back in 1776, the Founding Fathers wrote in the Declaration of Independence:

We hold these truths to be self-evident, that all men are created equal, that they are endowed by their Creator with certain unalienable Rights, that among these are Life, Liberty and the pursuit of Happiness.

What makes you happy? How often would you say you pursue happiness? Has that pursuit been fruitful?

When is a time your search for happiness turned out differently than you expected?

The founders of the United States believed the good life was ours for the taking if only we could catch it and keep it. But catching it is like chasing shadows. No matter how fast we run, it always seems to be just beyond our reach. After a while, we stop reaching and just settle. The truth isn't that happiness is unattainable, but that we're searching for happiness in places we can never hope to find it.

THE SURPRISING PATH TO HAPPINESS

Jesus is the happiest person who ever walked this earth (we'll return to this thought in the next personal study), and He gave us a manifesto on happiness in a set of teachings known as the Beatitudes. He began this way:

Blessed are the poor in spirit,
for the kingdom of heaven is theirs.
MATTHEW 5:3

What's your response to this teaching? Is it comforting? confusing? something else?

How does Jesus' teaching contrast with what the world teaches us about happiness?

The world tells us we achieve happiness through what we have: lots of friends, a cool car, good grades, a college scholarship. Those are all good, but Jesus says the path to the good life begins with having nothing.

In the language of the New Testament, the word translated "poor" was commonly used to describe beggars who depended on providers. In the Old Testament, the word implied hope in God alone. Jesus is teaching us that the good life is only for beggars. In other words, the good life is only available to those who realize everything they need comes from God.

But if that's all it takes to be happy, why are so many of us unhappy? What keeps us from being happy? The answer is simple: our pride.

THE FORK IN THE PATH

Read Genesis 1:26-31; 2:7-9,15-25; and 3:1-7.

How had God provided for the man and woman in the garden?

God breathed divine life into Adam and Eve, and as they carried on their lives in the garden, they showed their confidence and reliance on God Himself. He was their source and purpose. He promised to sustain their lives and give them purpose, and they promised to obey God by relying on Him, cultivating the garden, and multiplying His image. They had the good life.

If Adam and Eve had the good life, why did they disobey God's command?

Satan lied to Adam and Eve, tempting them with a distorted vision of the good life. They were already living it, but he led them to believe God was holding out on them. Eating from the Tree of the Knowledge of Good and Evil was an act of rebellion. It was the most vicious form of pride, saying, "God, I don't need you."

How does our pride keep us from becoming "poor in spirit"?

God created human beings to rely on Him, but in an act of pride, Adam and Eve chose to be self-reliant. Eve believed the lie that she knew better than God. The Scripture tells us she took the fruit because she saw the tree was "*good* for food and *delightful* to look at, and that it was *desirable* for obtaining wisdom" (3:6, emphasis mine). She thought taking from the tree would make her happy, but it resulted in misery. Her pride took her away from happiness. And we still feel the effects of that sin today. Sin results in physical and spiritual death and creates a debt we can never repay.

THE PRIDE DEBT

Read Romans 5:12.

How did Adam and Eve's sin extend to all of us?

Where do you feel the effects of this in your daily life?

We can't live the good life when we're wrapped up in our sinfulness. Adam and Eve chose slavery over freedom, and now we're born into slavery and in need of rescuing. We need to be restored to the good life God designed for us.

Read Romans 5:17.

How did God rescue and restore us to the good life?

The average cost of a college degree has skyrocketed in the last 30 years. In 1989, tuition at the average public four-year university cost about $3,500 per year. In 2019? $10,440.[1] Total student loan debt in the U.S. has now topped $1.41 trillion—an amount big enough on its own to be one of the 15 biggest economies in the world.[2]

Imagine if someone paid off all that debt at once. Our sin debt was bigger—a deeper and more crippling debt than anything we could ever hope to pay. And God stepped into the middle of that debt, nailed it to a cross, and forgave it. Happy are those who let God pay off their sin debt!

BACK ON THE PATH TO HAPPINESS

Read the following verses.

He erased the certificate of debt, with its obligations, that was against us and opposed to us, and has taken it away by nailing it to the cross.
COLOSSIANS 2:14

How joyful is the one whose transgression is forgiven, whose sin is covered!
PSALM 32:1

Why should realizing what God has done for us lead us to be poor in spirit?

How does realizing what God has done for us lead us to true happiness?

Only spiritual beggars who realize they're completely dependent on God will inherit the kingdom Jesus spoke of. The only life worth having comes to us through the blood of Jesus for the forgiveness of our sins. We unlock the good life when we discover that it can only be found by being in a right relationship with God.

Prayer

Father God, life, liberty, and true happiness are only available in You. Help us come to You with humble and open arms. Allow us to receive Your life-changing grace. We're delighted to be beggars in Your kingdom.

THE HAPPIEST MAN WHO EVER LIVED

In this week's video teaching, you heard me say, "Jesus of Nazareth was the happiest person to have ever lived." In today's personal study we'll examine this statement a little closer. Because if Jesus truly is the happiest person who ever lived, to embrace the good life means that we need to align our hearts with His.

When you picture Jesus, do you imagine him as happy? Why or why not?

What made Jesus happy?

Jesus embodied the good life. He's the prototype of what humanity was meant to be. The first Adam cursed humanity by his disobedience in the garden of Eden; Jesus, the last Adam, reversed the curse through His obedience. The first Adam brought us death; the last Adam brought us back to life.

No matter the situation, Jesus had transcendent happiness that gave Him confidence and purpose. His happiness rooted Him in something deeper, better, and more beautiful than His circumstances. Jesus' circumstances weren't the cause of His happiness, nor did they add or subtract. Only spiritual beggars who realize they're completely dependent on God will inherit the kingdom. His happiness was a different kind of joy that seemed to come from a realm beyond ours. Here's how the author of Hebrews described it:

> *For the joy that lay before him, he endured the cross, despising the shame, and sat down at the right hand of the throne of God.*
> **HEBREWS 12:2**

**How was Jesus able to find happiness even
in a terrible and torturous situation?**

Jesus was able to find happiness even in dire circumstances. Even though Jesus was "a man of suffering" (Isa. 53:3), He was truly happy because He was truly human. He is the only person to live without sin, which distorts our humanity. Salvation restores our humanity. Through Jesus, we gain the capacity to experience real happiness, the God-kind-of-happiness He reserves for citizens of His kingdom.

Jesus is the embodiment of the Beatitudes. He was humble and poor. His short time on earth had lasting endurance because He spent it pursuing God's justice and righteousness. Jesus, the Prince of peace, brought the peace of God everywhere He went. The cross transformed enemies into friends, failures into successes, and cowards into conquering apostles.

And He still invites people to be happy. According to Jesus, the blessed—or happy—are those whose lives are supernaturally interwoven into Jesus' life, and who are participating in His kingdom by the Holy Spirit's power. Our lives are transformed as we become more like Him.

FINDING JESUS THROUGH THE WORD

**Spend a few moments praying through and meditating
on these verses and those on the next page.**

*I am the vine; you are the branches. The one who remains in me and I
in him produces much fruit because you can do nothing without me.*
JOHN 15:5

*I have been crucified with Christ, and I no longer live, but
Christ lives in me. The life I now live in the body, I live by faith
in the Son of God, who loved me and gave himself for me.*
GALATIANS 2:20

I labor for this, striving with his strength that works powerfully in me.
COLOSSIANS 1:29

*For it is God who is working in you both to will and
to work according to his good purpose.*
PHILIPPIANS 2:13

*Now to him who is able to do above and beyond all that we ask or
think according to the power that works in us—to him be glory in the
church and in Christ Jesus to all generations, forever and ever. Amen.*
EPHESIANS 3:20-21

What does it mean to be crucified with Christ?

**Pick one of these verses and read it closely—what does it teach
you about your need to rely on Jesus? Memorize it this week.**

**What is one area of your life you need to begin trusting
and relying on Jesus rather than yourself?**

Only the poor in spirit—spiritual beggars—are welcome in the King's kingdom. At the entrance to Jesus' kingdom is a sign that reads, "Only beggars past this point." We should thank God every day for the privilege of being a beggar.

Prayer

Jesus, thank You for saving us when we couldn't save ourselves. Would you please, by Your Spirit, help us to depend on You every day? As we do that, would You supernaturally allow Your life and Your happiness to flow through us to others? In Your name we pray. Amen.

HAPPINESS 101

Who is the happiest person you know?
What makes them happy?

In 2000, fifty books were written on the topic of happiness. Eight years later, 4,000 books were written on it.[3] "According to some measures, as a nation we've grown sadder and more anxious during the same years that the happiness movement has flourished,"[4] wrote Carlin Flora of *Psychology Today*. To highlight the unhappiness in our culture, Yale University now offers a class on the subject that has become the most popular class in the prestigious school's history. Almost 25 percent of Yale's undergrads take the course, Psyc 157, Psychology and the Good Life. Dr. Laurie Santos, who teaches it, writes, "Students want to change, to be happier themselves, and to change the culture here on campus."[5]

In their search, many are learning all the places where it can't be found: relationships, sex, achievements, championships, or anything else. C.S. Lewis, a former atheist who became one of the most beloved Christians of the twentieth century, was on to something when he wrote:

> *If I find in myself a desire which no experience in this world can satisfy, the most probable explanation is that I was made for another world. If none of my earthly pleasures satisfy it, that does not prove that the universe is a fraud. Probably earthly pleasures were never meant to satisfy it, but only to arouse it, to suggest the real thing.*[6]

Lewis discovered what King David discovered long before Him. True happiness can only be found in God. David once said:

> *You reveal the path of life to me; in your presence is abundant joy; at your right hand are eternal pleasures.*
> **PSALM 16:11**

Solomon, David's son, once wrote that people make the choices that seem right to them (Prov. 14:12). When we see people seeking happiness in the wrong places, that's what they're doing—choosing a path that seems right to them. Most of the time, they aren't aware it will be unfulfilling. As disciples of Jesus, we have the opportunity to enter into these relationships and help people find what we've found—that the good life comes to us when we become beggars before God.

Whom do you know who is seeking the good life in all the wrong places? What can you do to show them the way to Jesus?

If you could write a short definition for "happiness," what would it be?

Whom can you pray for this week that needs Jesus' true happiness?

Prayer

Holy Spirit, please help me to see people as You see them—as people whom God loves desperately and who need the same grace I've received.

1. *CollegeBoard*, "Trends in College Pricing, 2019." https://research.collegeboard.org/trends/college-pricing; (Accessed March 9, 2020).
2. Daniel Kurt, "Student Loan Debt: 2019 Statistics and Outlook." *Investopedia*, https://www.investopedia.com/student-loan-debt-2019-statistics-and-outlook-4772007; (Accessed March 9,2020).
3. Carlin Flora, "The Pursuit of Happiness." *Psychology Today*, https://www.psychologytoday.com/us/articles/200901/the-pursuit-happiness; (Accessed June 12, 2019).
4. Ibid.
5. David Shimmer, "Yale's Most Popular Class Ever: Happiness." *The New York Times*, https://www.nytimes.com/2018/01/26/nyregion/at-yale-class-on-happiness-draws-huge-crowd-laurie-santos.html; (Accessed June 20, 2019).
6. C. S. Lewis, *Mere Christianity* (San Francisco: Harper Collins, 1952), 136-137.

Week 2
the good life

HAPPY ARE THOSE WHO

Lament

WELCOME TO SESSION 2

Think back to last week. What was your most significant takeaway about what it means to be "poor in spirit"?

Last week we learned what it means to be a spiritual beggar. This week we'll continue our walk through the Beatitudes, and we're going to see that true happiness comes to those who lament.

When was the last time you experienced something painful? How did you react to it?

So much of what Jesus taught was counter-cultural. His thoughts on happiness are no different. In this session, we will see that those who lament are joyful because they are cemented in God's comfort.

Use this space to take notes during the video teaching.

Discuss

Read Jesus' words together.

Blessed are those who mourn,
for they will be comforted.
MATTHEW 5:4

Why is it that instead of lamenting or mourning we try to rush through pain? What does this say about us?

How does mourning enhance our capacity to receive God's comfort?

Read Psalm 34:18. How have you felt God's presence in the midst of pain?

What does it look like to mourn sin, evil, injustice, suffering, and tragedy? How does mourning lead us to comfort from God?

How does God want to use our pain for a purpose?

How can lamenting connect us to others who suffer?

OVER THE NEXT WEEK
Marinate on This

Those who lament will be cemented in God's comfort.

God's greatest goal, His unrelenting aim
and passion, is to form Christ in us.

Suffering produces endurance. Endurance leads to
proven character. Proven character produces hope
because God pours His love into our hearts.

To heal our brokenness, God lovingly entered
our suffering and was broken on a cross.

Pain sends us into our purpose. Out of broken hearts we cry out
to God, and His comforting grace moves us to comfort others.

Jesus' accomplishments and obedience are applied to us.

Biblical lament means allowing your heart to be broken by the
same things that break God's heart, knowing all the while that
God is near the brokenhearted. Lament moves us to action.

Blessed are

THOSE WHO MOURN,

for they will be comforted.

MATTHEW 5:4

HAPPY ARE THE SAD?

As Jesus continued to teach with His disciples sitting at His feet, Matthew records Him saying,

Blessed are those who mourn, for they will be comforted.
MATTHEW 5:4

The Greek word translated here as "mourn" is the strongest word for mourning or lamenting in the New Testament. It expresses loud crying, as though someone were wailing in agony over sin, suffering, injustice, and human tragedy. It describes a person whose heart is broken by what breaks God's heart.

This might be the most counterintuitive Beatitude.
Does it seem odd to you that Jesus says we're
"blessed" when we mourn? Why or why not?

Anyone who follows the news knows there is plenty in the world to lament. To lament is to agree with God about the sin and disruption in the world and mourn its presence. Lamenting is different than complaining, which is selfish in nature and assigns God blame for our misgivings.

Give an example of a lament and a complaint.
Which one do you gravitate to more often?

Lamenting the way things are is tied to longing for the way things ought to be. As Christians, we should long for a world that the gospel has cured—one where God's kingdom in Christ has completely invaded. Before we can be on mission living in and for God's kingdom, we must lament the idolatry and injustice of the world.

What's happening in the world right now that breaks your heart? It can be something in your own life or something on the other side of the world.

A FIRST-CENTURY EXAMPLE

Taking a look at the New Testament world helps us understand what Jesus meant when He said the good life is found by mourning. First-century Jewish people had much to mourn. The pagan, idol-worshiping Romans dominated and oppressed God's people in the promised land. Injustice was like a bad odor filling the air, polluting both Jews and Gentiles alike.

Rome was brutal toward the Jews, and many in the elite Jewish religious class were brutal to Jews of lower social status. The Jewish religious establishment considered the sinners, the chronically sick, and the tax collectors unclean, so Jewish law forbade them to participate in Jewish religious life. Jesus comforted the rejected and the mourners. A rabbi would never share a meal with the unclean, but Jesus was different. He was the Messiah. He didn't have to preserve His cleanliness from the unclean; He made the unclean, clean.

How does understanding this context help you appreciate Jesus' words more fully?

One of those who received Jesus' comfort was the former tax collector, Matthew. What would it have been like to witness Jesus and Matthew's meal? Matthew recounted the experience in Matthew 9.

Read Matthew 9:10-13.

What was it about Jesus that made "sinners and tax collectors" feel comfortable coming to Him?

What did these sinners see in Jesus that the Pharisees missed?

Jesus is the doctor who performs surgery with a scalpel called mercy. He doesn't write healing prescriptions in ink, but in His blood. Sadly, many of the Jewish religious leaders weren't interested in Jesus' cure, so they pursued a homemade remedy of religiosity that only made them more hostile toward Jesus. Many of the Pharisees and Sadducees, two leading Jewish religious groups, were known for their religious sacrifices but not for giving mercy to sinners and outcasts. Jesus mourned over the religious leaders' rejection of Him (Matt. 23:37-39). They failed to mourn their own sin and the effects of sin in the world around them.

Jesus lamented how the Pharisees and Sadducees were hypocrites who shut the door of the kingdom of heaven in people's faces, preventing their entry (Matt. 23:13). He lamented how the dark power had corrupted those who were to lead the people into God's kingdom, and that they were themselves whitewashed tombs, a brood of vipers, full of greed, and self-indulgence (Matt. 23:15-29). True lament requires we recognize and mourn the sin hidden in our hearts. The Jewish leaders failed to do that and so do we. Jesus yearned to gather the Jewish people under His wings, but like the prophets of old, He was rejected and ultimately nailed to a cross. True lament brings God's comfort.

DIFFERENT TAX COLLECTOR, SAME SAVIOR

Read Luke 18:9-14.

**In this parable, which person embraced
what Jesus taught in Matthew 5:4?**

**Which character best represents your attitude toward
your sin: the Pharisee or the tax collector? Why?**

Luke's Gospel recounts a teaching of Jesus to "some who trusted in themselves that they were righteous and looked down on everyone else" (v. 9). In this teaching Jesus makes an unlikely comparison. The Pharisees were known for their devout religious practices. But by examining one Pharisee's prayer life, Jesus exposed it as a proud performance before a crowd. What was so clear to the tax collector, the Pharisee failed to see: that he was the one who needed saving.

The tax collector lamented—expressing genuine, chest-beating sorrow over his sin-sickness and looked to God as the only cure. If the point of this parable wasn't clear enough, Jesus concluded this way:

> *I tell you, this one went down to his house justified rather
> than the other; because everyone who exalts himself will be
> humbled, but the one who humbles himself will be exalted.*
> **LUKE 18:14**

Because sin breaks God's heart, it should break ours as well. Failure to lament produces a spiritual pride that keeps us from embracing the God-dependent spiritual poverty we learned about in the last session. Pride causes us to see those with needs around us as "others" who should be avoided rather than strugglers who need God's comfort.

GOD'S COMFORT FOR THOSE WHO MOURN

Marinate in God's promises to those who mourn.

The Spirit of the Lord GOD is on me,
because the LORD has anointed me
to bring good news to the poor.
He has sent me to heal the brokenhearted,
to proclaim liberty to the captives
and freedom to the prisoners;
to proclaim the year of the LORD's favor,
and the day of our God's vengeance;
to comfort all who mourn,
to provide for those who mourn in Zion;
to give them a crown of beauty instead of ashes,
festive oil instead of mourning,
and splendid clothes instead of despair.
ISAIAH 61:1-3

According to these verses, what does Jesus promise to those who lament?

In Luke 4:18-19, we see that Jesus read these words in the synagogue, declaring them to be about Him. But the salvation Jesus brings isn't only about saving us from our sins. Jesus' ministry also points towards a messianic age of restoration, healing, and comfort. These promises are a declaration that we can be happy as we lament because our lament will cement us in God's comfort.

Prayer

Father God, thank You for sending Jesus to comfort the afflicted. May our mourning lead us into a deeper experience of your transforming grace.

LAMENTING POINTS TO JESUS

The second Beatitude can be hard for us to embrace because when we're lamenting, comfort seems too far off. When comfort seems far away, we believe the lie that God is far away. So what is Jesus doing during our lamenting, and how is it driving us closer to Him? This is what we're diving into today. Through the apostle Paul, we see how pain works in our lives.

Read Romans 5:3-5.

ENDURANCE

God doesn't waste our pain. It's as though God takes our pain and uses it to purify us. During suffering, God graciously grants us access to the suffering of Christ Jesus. His endurance becomes ours. In our weakness, His strength becomes ours. He becomes our fortress of hope as we grow our roots deeper and deeper into the soil of His great love.

When was a time you had to show great endurance?

PROVEN CHARACTER

The endurance wrought by suffering leads to proven character. God's greatest goal, His unrelenting aim and passion, is to form Christ in us. Just like training an athlete, God in His sovereign love allows the brokenness of this world to be a tool in His nail-pierced hands to heal our broken character. Through the flames of suffering, He forges our character to reflect Jesus': As we press into Jesus, His character becomes our character. As we press into Him we become like Him.

How has walking through pain helped you grow in Christlikeness? How does this help you see pain differently?

HOPE

Proven character produces hope because God pours His love into our hearts. It's quite a mystery that suffering expands our capacity to understand how much God loves us. In suffering, we get a glimpse of how Jesus suffered for the sins of the world. The only reason there is cancer, disease, depression, anxiety, and other forms of pain is that creation itself is broken and longing to be rescued from decay and corruption. Creation is fallen and in need of redemption just like humanity. The cross of Jesus will eventually even heal creation (Rom. 8:18-29).

Read Romans 8:28-30. How does knowing Jesus give us hope even in pain?

Hope has a name, and it's Jesus. Through His cross and resurrection, our bodies, along with all of creation, will be made whole. But until that time, God lovingly enters our suffering. Jesus was broken on a cross to heal our brokenness. Our hope isn't a mere wish but an assurance because God through the Holy Spirit is pouring His love into our hearts.

Prayer

Lord Jesus, thank You for using everything in life—even my pain—to conform me into Your image. We praise You that even when we might not understand all that's happening to us we know God is working through us.

LAMENT INTO ACTION

LAMENT DURING PERSONAL STRUGGLES

Describe a time when you saw someone in pain and helped them. What made you feel like you needed to act?

The more time we spend sitting at Jesus' feet and learning from Him, the more we're connected to His heart. And in a way that only He understands, He transforms us into better people because our love for people and their struggles increases. If we're truly following Jesus, our laments should look like His. Lament should lead us to action because God is a God of action. King David wrote about God's action toward those in pain in the psalms:

> *The LORD is near the brokenhearted;*
> *he saves those crushed in spirit.*
> **PSALM 34:18**

When have you felt God's presence in your pain?

How are we modeling God's character when we care for our friends who are struggling?

Lamenting is a holy hurt. But the hurt is a pain that pushes us deeper into faith, hope, and love. It pushes us deeper into our faith in Jesus and His redemptive purposes and deeper into hope, which is the knowledge that one day all things will be made new.

In the midst of human suffering, having someone who cares for you, comforts you, prays with you, reads Scripture over you, and nurtures you through the rising river of pain is a gift. It's as if God heals us as we become instruments of healing touch.

Whom do you know who is in pain and could use someone to care for them in the name of Jesus? What can you do to help them?

THE SINS WE SHARE

It feels natural to mourn over our own sins—it leads to repentance and praise because the blood of Jesus wiped away our sins. They're nailed to the cross and left there forever. We are not so good, however, at acknowledging and lamenting the sins we all share.

Why is it important that we continue to confess our sins, even knowing that Jesus already died on the cross for them?

Nothing is more individualistic than social media. From Instagram to TikTok, every moment we experience is another opportunity to bare our lives to the world in return for a few likes. We see the world through a selfish lens. The Bible, however, corrects our individualism. We are unique people, but we're also part of a community. The moment we're born again, it's into a community— the Church. We have a corporate identity, not just an individual one.

We see this in the Old Testament through the people of Israel who were designed to be a "light to the nations" (Isa. 42:6), and in the New Testament with God's new covenant community, the Church. How we live in community matters. Therefore, when the Church sins, we need to lament and repent not just individually, but together.

Read Matthew 6:12. Why does Jesus use "us" and "our" in this prayer? Have you ever thought of the shared element of sin? .

The Bible calls followers of Jesus the body of Christ (1 Cor. 12:27), so the way we live reflects on all of us. As followers of Jesus, it's vital to our discipleship that we learn to lament shared sin because lament moves us to action. What does this action look like?

First, we ask the Holy Spirit to search our own hearts so we may repent of our personal sins. Second, we ask Jesus to start a revival in our own individual lives. Third, we come together to confess our sins and ask forgiveness from the people we've hurt. Fourth, we make restitution to those we've wronged. We try to right our wrongs. Fifth, we seek to hold pastors and leaders in the church responsible and accountable to hurtful actions. Sixth, church leaders must teach and equip their congregations, because lament moves us to action.

What are some things we need to repent for as the body of Christ? How can we be better? What will you do to help?

Prayer

Holy Spirit, thank You for making us one body in Christ. Help us to see sin as You do and repent for it together, because lament moves us to action.

Week 3
the good life

HAPPY ARE THE

Humble

Start

WELCOME TO SESSION 3

**During the last week as you were challenged
to see how our lament leads to our happiness,
what was your most significant takeaway?**

Last week's study challenged us to see the surprising connection between lament and the good life. This week we'll focus on humility.

**Think back to a time when you were humbled—
maybe it was a bad grade on a test or a crucial
mistake in a game. How did you feel?**

Jesus said happiness is found in humility. At first, that might be hard to believe. Humility can be difficult. But true humility doesn't call attention to itself—it focuses away from itself toward others. Today, we're going to examine humility from God's perspective.

Watch

Use this space to take notes during the video teaching.

Discuss

Read Jesus' words together.

*Blessed are the humble,
for they will inherit the earth.*
MATTHEW 5:5

Peter went from being a denier of the faith to a defender of the faith. How can you relate to Peter? Have you experienced moments of weakness in your faith?

How have you, like Peter, been humbled and transformed through knowing Jesus?

In the video Pastor Derwin said, "God only uses normal people, because that's all He has to work with." Who is an example of a "normal person" God used in the Bible?

Would you say most people show humility in their day-to-day lives?

When has God accomplished something through you that you could've never accomplished on your own? Why should this make you humble?

How can you cultivate true humility in your life?

OVER THE NEXT WEEK
Marinate on This

Humility is placing yourself under the
grace, glory, and mission of God.

Humility gives us supernatural abilities
to accomplish God's mission.

The more we see God's holiness, the more humble we
become. The more we see our sin, the more we appreciate
God's grace, and the more we desire to obey Jesus.

Grace forms a partnership between Jesus and
us to be about His kingdom business.

Through His grace, Jesus gives us the
ability to obey as He requires.

Blessed are

THE HUMBLE,

for they will inherit the earth.

MATTHEW 5:5

HUMILITY REIMAGINED

THE CALL

How would you define humility?

How often do you think about being humble?

Never   **All the time**

We often think humility is timidity, shyness, or even weakness. But we're wrong. The humility God imparts to us takes root in the soil of our souls, and as we water and fertilize it by faith, courage and conviction begin to grow in us. We become stronger because our confidence is in God, not ourselves. Instead of having self-confidence, we have Godfidence.

How did Jesus display humility?

Think about it: Jesus wasn't timid, shy, or weak, yet He was the most humble man who ever lived. Why? Because He fully trusted in and depended on His Father. Humility isn't weakness. Humility is placing yourself under the grace, glory, love, and mission of God. In our humility we tap into God's power.

The disciples heard Jesus teach, "Blessed are the humble, for they will inherit the earth (Matt. 5:5). The Greek word translated *humble* (or *meek* in some translations) conveys the idea of power that's under control. It's like a horse that has learned to listen the commands of its rider. Jesus is saying happy are those whose power is found in God, not themselves.

THE REWARD

To "inherit the earth" simply means to gain citizenship and authority under God in the new heavens and new earth. God will populate His new creation with humble people. After the resurrection of humanity, everyone in the new heavens and new earth will only brag about Jesus. Eternity will have one boast: "Worthy is the Lamb" (Rev. 5:12).

In your own words, what do you think it means to "inherit the earth"?

What is your reaction when you hear someone bragging? What does God want us to brag about?

Why is being humble so difficult?

Lack of humility is rooted in pride. It's like a weed that creeps into our hearts and chokes out the healthy seeds of humility waiting to germinate. When we feel like we're losing the battle between humility and pride, we find good company in the first disciples. They lived alongside Jesus every day for years, but even toward the end of Jesus' earthly ministry their actions showed they hadn't fully grasped His humility.

HUMILITY IN ACTION

Read Luke 22:14-16,24-30.

Jesus had walked with and trained His students for three years, but now it was time for Him to die for the sins of the world. In that moment, pride arose like a serpent among the disciples (v. 24). Jesus used this moment before His death to teach and model humility for His disciples.

Do you identify with the disciples' desire to be seen as great? What correction does Jesus offer for that desire?

Jesus taught about humility and lived a life of humility, yet the disciples began to argue about who would be the greatest in God's kingdom. Clearly, they were still missing the heart of Jesus' teaching on humility. Jesus then did the unthinkable: He washed the feet of the disciples.

Read John 13:1-5.

Why was washing the disciples' feet such a radical gesture?

Washing feet was the task of a household servant. Jesus was performing the task of a slave. The humility of God is overwhelming. How could God the Son wash the feet of disciples who were arguing about who would be the greatest? Once again, Jesus didn't run out of grace and patience with His disciples, and as we experience Jesus' grace and patience, we become humble enough to serve others well.

Have you felt Jesus leading you to be more humble? If so, what is He teaching you? If not, how can you pray for it?

In God's economy, great people are humble enough to become great servants. Instead of living for others to serve us, we live to serve others as an act of worship. We move from being self-centered to others-centered, because our lives are centered on Jesus.

Is our culture self-centered or others-centered? Where do you see this the most?

In first century Greco-Roman society, the Romans didn't value humility. Judaism for the most part did. In the Greco-Roman world, humility was weakness. In the Jewish world, it was a virtue. In washing His disciples' feet, Jesus overturned the social status: the king performed the task of the servant. He was embodying the beauty of humility. The greatest among you should be the greatest servants—that's the way of the kingdom.

Where do you need to shed your pride in order to sacrifice for the sake of others?

End your time today by meditating on the humility of Christ.

Adopt the same attitude as that of Christ Jesus,
who, existing in the form of God,
did not consider equality with God
as something to be exploited.
Instead he emptied himself
by assuming the form of a servant,
taking on the likeness of humanity.
And when he had come as a man,
he humbled himself by becoming obedient
to the point of death—
even to death on a cross.
For this reason God highly exalted him
and gave him the name
that is above every name,
so that at the name of Jesus
every knee will bow—
in heaven and on earth
and under the earth—
and every tongue will confess
that Jesus Christ is Lord,
to the glory of God the Father.
PHILIPPIANS 2:5-11

Happy are the humble, for they're the ones becoming like Jesus.

Prayer

Jesus, help us to be people marked by humility. Help our hearts to become like Yours, so we would pursue greatness through servant-hearted self-denial.

DENIER THEN DEFENDER

PETER THE DENIER

In your journey with Jesus, what circumstances have helped you learn humility?

Out of all of Jesus' disciples, Peter is most often the stand-in for us. At moments he was loyal, dependable, and wise. At other moments, he was running from servant girls who questioned him about knowing Jesus. Peter at times was brave enough to walk on water, and at other times his bravery was severely lacking. There's a little of Peter in all of us.

Peter learned humility and Christlike service by being humiliated. He had to be shaped by difficult circumstances. As Jesus was preparing for the cross, He told His disciples they would abandon Him. Peter boldly responded that even if everyone else abandoned Him, he never would (Matt. 26:33,35). Jesus told Peter that he would deny Him not just once but three times that night (Matt. 26:34). As Jesus was being led like a lamb to slaughter, Matthew records Peter's actions.

Read Matthew 26:74-75.

How do you identify with Peter in this moment?

When has pride, weakness, or self-preservation caused you to deny Jesus?

Peter cried at the memory of what Jesus told him. He was confronted with the reality of his weakness, which we all share. We're prone to blowing it when we place our confidence in our strength instead of God's.

**What's one area where you need to rely on
God's strength instead of your own?**

At any moment, any of us, like Peter, can make a shipwreck out of our lives. This is why we all need God's sin-defeating grace imparted to us through communion with the Holy Spirit. As we depend upon the Holy Spirit, God's strength shines through our weakness.

PETER THE DEFENDER

Peter thought too highly of himself, and then in the crucible of life he denied Jesus. But Peter's life was changed by the Holy Spirit. The same man who denied Jesus also wrote a beautiful call to humility.

Read 1 Peter 5:6-7.

**Compare Peter's words with Matthew 5:5.
How are these passages similar?**

How does our connection to Jesus enable us to be humble?

Humility allows us to access Jesus' supernatural ability to defeat sin and adversity. Eventually, Jesus restored Peter and sent Him on mission. Peter was a pillar of the early church and gave his life for the sake of the gospel. Jesus radically changed this proud, unpredictable disciple. The good life is a humble life of leaning on Jesus. The same Spirit working in Peter works in us today. We can ask Him to make us humbly dependent on God.

THE SPIRIT AT WORK IN US

The work of the Holy Spirit has changed us, like Peter, from deniers to defenders.

Spend a few moments meditating on the following Scriptures using these questions as a guide.

God resists the proud,
but gives grace to the humble,
Therefore, submit to God. Resist the devil, and he will flee
from you. Draw near to God, and he will draw near to you.
JAMES 4:6-8

Humility is ultimately submission to God. Where do you need to submit to God's leadership?

Therefore, as God's chosen ones, holy and dearly loved, put on
compassion, kindness, humility, gentleness, and patience.
COLOSSIANS 3:12

Pick one other trait mentioned in this verse. What does it mean to you?

How does being humble lead to these other traits?

Mankind, he has told each of you what is good
and what it is the LORD requires of you:
to act justly,
to love faithfulness,
and to walk humbly with your God.
MICAH 6:8

Why must you be humble to act justly and love faithfulness? Are these traits evident in your life?

What is the Holy Spirit teaching you about humility through these Scriptures?

Prayer

Holy Spirit, lead us to see God more clearly. Lead us into the humble confidence that comes from trusting that God knows us, loves us, and has called us to live under His rule.

RESISTING PRIDE

We have seen throughout this study how the good life should impact our relationships. Pride is the antithesis of humility. When we give in to our pride, we sin against God and others. At the end of this week, consider two big questions.

Is there any area of your life where you're being too prideful? Take a few moments in prayer to confess your sin and receive forgiveness.

Is there any sinful pride disrupting your relationship with a brother or sister in Christ? Find a time to speak with them and request their forgiveness.

Prayer

Lord Jesus, thank You for humbling Yourself to the point of death on a cross. Please convict us of our pride, replace our pride with humility, and allow us to receive the cleansing power of Your blood.

Week 4
the good life

HAPPY ARE THE
Hungry
& Thirsty

Start

WELCOME TO SESSION 4

**How have you felt challenged during the last
week to let go of pride and embrace humility?
What was your most significant takeaway?**

This week we're going to take a look at our innate desires for justice and righteousness.

What's an injustice in the world you long to see made right?

In this session, we will see that the heartache we all experience when we see hurt and injustice in the world is actually a longing for the good life that God has promised to us in Christ.

Watch

Use this space to take notes during the video teaching.

Discuss

Read Jesus' words together.

Blessed are those who hunger and thirst for righteousness,
for they will be filled.
MATTHEW 5:6

How did Jesus enter into our broken world and display God's righteousness?

God sent Jesus to join us in our brokenness and meet our deepest needs. Why should this compel us to meet others' needs?

Give an example of a time Jesus' heart broke for another person. How did it drive Him to action?

In this week's video, you heard the story of Manny Ohonme, who was moved to start a ministry to bring God's righteousness and goodness to the world. How can you do this in your own life?

The word translated *filled* means "full to overflowing." How does thirsting and hungering for righteousness satisfy our souls?

Pastor Derwin said, "God doesn't need your ability. He needs your availability." How can you join God in displaying His righteousness in this broken world?

OVER THE NEXT WEEK
Marinate on This

We are God's agents of grace and redemption.

The King of heaven gives you His righteousness so you can express it to the world around you.

Happiness is found in becoming God's paintbrush to create beauty where there's ugliness, hope where there's despair, and salvation where there's death.

God isn't looking for your ability; He longs for your availability to share His supernatural ability.

The good life looks like a life of repentance, forgiveness, mercy, and serving the hurting.

God takes unrighteous people and makes them righteous through the blood of Christ, so they can express His righteousness to the earth.

Blessed are

THOSE WHO HUNGER AND THIRST FOR RIGHTEOUSNESS,

for they will be filled.

MATTHEW 5:6

FEELING THE NEED

Do you ever have trouble reconciling the "bad" of this world with the existence of God? Explain.

Have you been able to work through that tension? What conclusions have you drawn?

It's easy to become overwhelmed with the world's injustices. School shootings fill the news, while wars and humanitarian crises rage overseas. Religious leaders—who are supposed to represent Christ—cover up abuse instead. Children are displaced by war and conflict; families are separated while seeking safety. We live in a broken, grieving world, and it's easy to succumb to the magnitude of its needs.

Perhaps prolific injustice has even led some of us to wonder how there can really be a powerful, loving God if there's so much ugliness in the world. If you find yourself there today, keep reading. Whether or not you realize it now, your anger, disappointment, and desire for this world to be redeemed show that you long for the beauty of God. Consider this question:

How do we know something is unjust unless we believe there's a standard of justice?

If we long for goodness, beauty, and justice, there must be one who created these things. That Creator must exhibit those things because we can't give away what we don't possess. As we yell and shake our fists at all the wrongs in the world, we're longing for God to make the sad things untrue, to make the ugly beautiful, to heal the hurt.

Read Psalm 33:5 and Amos 5:24.

How do we reflect God's character when we long for justice?

How does knowing God is righteous and just change the way you feel about the injustice you see around you?

The triune God made creation good, and we messed it up. We introduced death and decay, but God didn't leave us in our mess; He joined us in our brokenness. He even allowed all the sad things that have happened to us to happen to Him on the cross. His resurrection births a new creation in the heart of the old. The righteousness and justice we long for walked out of a tomb in Jerusalem. Through the power of the Holy Spirit, He wants us to become actors in the divine drama of redemption. We become His agents of redemption.

JESUS REDEFINES OUR NEEDS

Jesus continued to teach in the Sermon on the Mount:

Blessed are those who hunger and thirst for righteousness,
for they will be filled.
MATTHEW 5:6

Jesus took a common human feeling and connected it to God's kingdom. In the ancient world, food and water weren't as abundant as they are now. To thirst and hunger for righteousness was to love God with all your being and to love your neighbor the way you love yourself.

Just as a person can't live without food or water, we can't live without God. We were made to be fueled by God's life and love. He's the only food that will nourish us and the only drink that will satisfy our thirst. Jesus, the author of all Scripture, had Isaiah's words in mind:

> *Come, everyone who is thirsty,*
> *come to the water;*
> *and you without silver,*
> *come, buy, and eat!*
> *Come, buy wine and milk*
> *without silver and without cost!*
> ISAIAH 55:1

As you reflect on this verse, what comes to mind? Do you trust God to provide all you need? If not, why not?

The food and water we need to live and thrive is free of charge—we simply must come. It's a gift from His banquet table. He freely feeds us and gives us all we need to be conformed to the image of Christ, which happens as we feed on Christ.

Read John 6:48-51 and 7:37-38.

What did Jesus mean when He called Himself the "Bread of life" and "living Water"?

When did you first ask Jesus to meet your needs?

How is He meeting your needs right now?

In John's Gospel, Jesus compared our deepest physical needs (bread and water) to His ability to meet all our spiritual needs. Those who feast at Jesus' table will never be hungry or thirsty again (John 4:14). His stores have a limitless supply from which we eat until we're full.

JESUS FILLS US

Jesus says those who hunger and thirst for righteousness will be filled. The word "filled" means to be bloated or gorged. Happy are those who are so full of God that they can't help but tell everyone about Him.

Why should our love for God translate into a love for others?

The Scriptures connect our love for God to love for others (Matt. 22:37-39). If we find an amazing new show, we tell other people about it. We text our friends and say, "You have to watch this!" Similarly, when we experience the bounty of Christ's table, it should lead us to tell other people about it. God calls us to tell other people about His table.

There's plenty of room at God's banquet table—all the food and drink we want. God uses us to call other people to His table as we pursue His righteousness in the world.

Consider the following verse:

How happy are those who uphold justice,
who practice righteousness at all times.
PSALM 106:3

What does it look like to "practice righteousness"?
How is this connected to upholding justice?

How can you practice righteousness in your day-to-day life?

In this week's video session, I said, "Righteousness means God's justice and love is to be expressed through His people as a gift to the world." In other words, when God changes us, Christ's righteousness takes root in us, and we begin to pursue what's important to Jesus. When we hunger and thirst for righteousness, we are building God's kingdom. Happiness in Christ comes when we show an outward concern for meeting other people's needs and healing their hurts.

We'll consider what this looks like in the next two personal studies.

Prayer

Thank You, Father, for filling us with all the righteousness of Christ. We ask that You would lead us to hunger and thirst for Your righteousness. Help us to pursue justice in our communities and around the world.

GOD'S PAINTBRUSH

Think about this—people are praying right now, and God wants to use us to answer their prayers. The justice the world longs for is found in the church of Jesus Christ. The King of heaven gives us His righteousness, so we can express it to the world around us. If Jesus can lay down His life for us, who are we to keep our lives? Paradoxically, when we lay down our lives in service to others, we find the true good life. Jesus says,

> *If anyone wants to follow after me, let him deny himself, take up*
> *his cross daily, and follow me. For whoever wants to save his life*
> *will lose it, but whoever loses his life because of me will save it.*
> LUKE 9:23-24

How do Jesus' words sit with you? Are they
challenging? comforting? scary?

Happiness is found in righteousness. In pursuing justice in our communities and around the world. In meeting others' needs and healing their hurts. We find happiness in becoming God's paintbrush to create beauty where there's ugliness, hope where there's despair, and salvation where there's condemnation.

When have you experienced happiness through
meeting a need in the name of Jesus?

THE LIE WE BOUGHT

If finding the good life is this easy, why have so many Christians failed to find the good life? We've bought the lies that happiness is found in places we could never hope to find it. Instead of seeking His righteousness and His kingdom, we become consumed with building our own. When this happens we find heartbreak, not happiness. Consider Jesus' words from later in the Sermon on the Mount.

But seek first the kingdom of God and his righteousness,
and all these things will be provided for you.
MATTHEW 6:33

What promise does God make to us if we
make His kingdom our priority?

When is a time you put your own needs before someone else's?

Conversely, when was a time you put someone else's
needs before your own? What happened?

When we take our eyes off the kingdom of God and the righteousness it brings, our lives become insular and unsatisfying. Sure, we may be happy for a time, but we'll always find ourselves needing and wanting more. Only through Jesus can our truest hunger and thirst be filled. We seek Christ's kingdom as we pursue righteousness through meeting needs.

THE TRUTH WE NEED

Somewhere along the way, the church moved from a holistic view of pursuing righteousness and became unconcerned with the world around us. The Bible doesn't allow for such a disconnect. James wrote:

If a brother or sister is without clothes and lacks daily food and one of you says to them, "Go in peace, stay warm, and be well fed," but you don't give them what the body needs, what good is it? In the same way, faith, if it doesn't have works, is dead by itself.
JAMES 2:15-17

How is our personal righteousness connected to a genuine concern for others?

The term "works" that James uses expresses the idea that faith will compel us to love those in need (Jas. 2:8). True righteousness is always accompanied by a concern for others. God cares about the whole person and for all of humanity right here and now. We need to return to being the hands and feet of Jesus.

There is no shortage of opportunities to find places to bring God's love. Jesus is a holistic savior. He fed and healed people. Often, when Jesus met people's physical needs, they opened up to Him, and He then met their need for salvation also.

Prayer

God, please help us to see the needs in our community as You see them. Let the implanted righteousness You gave us through Your Son compel us to have a holistic concern for the world around us.

Outward

GOD'S ABILITY, YOUR AVAILABILITY

Our hunger and thirst for righteousness will compel us to meet needs in the world around us. Often these are right in our own neighborhood.

The good life answers God's call to make a positive difference in the world—to be a giver, not a taker. How different will the world be because we existed? We don't have to be in full-time ministry to make a difference—we just need to be faithful. God doesn't need our ability; He just wants our availability.

Here are some suggestions to get you started.

What is a need you're passionate about (homelessness, literacy, poverty, etc.)? Identify a few:

1.

2.

3.

Are there any ministries in your church or community meeting those needs? If so, when could you go serve with them?

If not, what would it look like to begin meeting those needs with your willingness to serve?

If you had trouble identifying a need, what are some ways you could begin to make a difference for people in your everyday life, at school and in your community?

How could you make serving and meeting needs a regular rhythm in your life?

How might these acts of service provide you opportunities to share Jesus with people who do not know Him?

If the people of God truly hungered and thirsted for God's righteousness, imagine all the good we could do. Let's pray that God would use us.

Prayer

Holy Spirit, bring us the needs of our community, trust us to meet them, and give us the grace to form relationships, so we can introduce others to Jesus.

Week 5
the good life

HAPPY ARE THE
Merciful

Start
WELCOME TO SESSION 5

**Last week, you were challenged to list ways
you could help meet your community's needs.
What ideas did you come up with?**

As we cross the halfway mark in our time in the Beatitudes, we're going to think together about how mercy makes us happy people.

**Share a time when someone showed
unexpected mercy toward you.**

In this session, we'll see that happiness and mercy go hand in hand. They're two sides of the same coin. The good life comes to us as we extend mercy to those in need.

. . . .
Use this space to take notes during the video teaching.
. . . .

Discuss

Read Jesus' words together.

Blessed are the merciful,
for they will be shown mercy.
MATTHEW 5:7

Jesus shares His mercy with us, so we may become merciful. How have you seen mercy at work in your life?

Mercy isn't afraid of human suffering. Who around you is suffering? How can you show them love?

Read Luke 10:25-37, and answer the following questions:

How was the good Samaritan merciful?

What does this parable teach us about the kind of mercy God desires from us?

How does God see people? How can you transform the way you see people?

How can you reach across cultural, ethnic, and generational lines to love someone different than you? How can you do that this week?

OVER THE NEXT WEEK
Marinate on This

Mercy Himself showed us a better way to be human.
Mercy isn't something God does; it's who He is.

Mercy is God presenting Himself to us in the midst of our mess.

We only know Jesus is merciful because He pursues us.

Jesus fights for us even when we're fighting against Him.

Mercy isn't afraid to cross ethnic,
cultural, and religious barriers.

Jesus' death and resurrection not only took the
punishment for our sins, but it also crucified the
various boundaries that separated us from God.

Mercy costs us something.

Blessed are

THE MERCIFUL,

for they will be shown mercy.

MATTHEW 5:7

MERCY CAME TO US

To define mercy, we need to look deeper into Jesus' teaching. As Jesus continues his manifesto on what it means to be happy, He says,

Blessed are the merciful,
for they will be shown mercy.
MATTHEW 5:7

How would you define mercy?

We all have ideas about what mercy is and isn't, but since mercy begins with God, we must look to His character to define it. Mercy isn't something God does; mercy is who God is.

GOD IS MERCY

Beginning in Exodus 19, Moses went up Mount Sinai to receive God's law. By the time Exodus 32 rolls around, Moses was still up on the mountain with God, and the Israelites decided to replace the leader God had given them with a golden calf. God's anger burned against the people in their sin (32:10) until Moses intervened. Mercifully, the Lord relented and reinstated His covenant with Israel. In this section, we find one of the great declarations of who God is.

Read Exodus 34:6-7.

How does God describe Himself in these verses? Make a list.

How is God's mercy reflected in this declaration?

God begins His declaration by saying He is merciful (some translations say compassionate). Once again we see God is mercy. It's essential to His being, which is eternal, infinite, and inexhaustible. God can no more run out of mercy than He can run out of Himself. In God's expression of His character, we also see two dimensions of mercy: forgiveness for the guilty and help for the needy.

MERCY FORGIVES THE GUILTY

Have you ever been forgiven when you didn't feel like you deserved it? How did you respond?

What must it have meant to Moses to hear that God is merciful right after the people He was leading had sinned so greatly?

On Mount Sinai, God showed Israel unmerited kindness. God's mercy inclines His face toward us with eyes of compassion and hands of tenderness. Mercy is God in Christ by the Spirit's power running toward humanity locked in a burning house of sin and death. Mercy breaks down the door and frees us from that burning house.

Read Ephesians 2:4-7. How has God revealed His mercy to us in Christ?

Mercy is God presenting himself to us in the midst of our mess. We only know Jesus is merciful because He pursues us. When we are lying helpless in a ditch He doesn't yell down and say, "Here's a ladder—climb up!" Jesus jumps into the pit with us, puts us on His back, and carries us out.

How have you continued to experience God's mercy in your walk with Him?

Jesus fights for us, even when we're fighting against Him. As Jesus identifies with our hurts, fears, and sins, we learn to "approach the throne of grace with boldness, so that we may receive mercy and find grace to help us in time of need" (Heb 4:16). God's mercy erases our past sins, is present help in our times of need, and assures that at the future judgment we will hear, "Therefore, there is now no condemnation for those in Christ Jesus" (Rom. 8:1). Jesus shares his mercy with us, so we can become merciful, and that leads to a second dimension of mercy.

HELP FOR THE NEEDY

In response to God's mercy, we extend mercy to others in need. When we were at our most needy, Christ came to us and rescued us from our spiritual poverty. Because Jesus gave of His resources, we freely give of what He has given us to help others in their times of need.

Read 2 Corinthians 8:9.

According to Paul, why should Christians extend themselves for others?

Read Matthew 22:37-39.

How is helping the needy connected to our obedience to the great commandment?

Merciful people love their neighbors. Mercy is an act of worship. We love God by loving people because we were also recipients of mercy. We don't give mercy to get mercy—that would be a business transaction. Mercy gives for the sake of mercy itself. This love looks like the cross of Jesus.

But when the kindness of God our Savior and his love for mankind appeared, he saved us—not by works of righteousness that we had done, but according to his mercy—through the washing of regeneration and renewal by the Holy Spirit.
TITUS 3:4-5

Is there someone in your life you need to show mercy to?

Prayer

Jesus, thank You for embodying mercy on the cross and giving to us when there's nothing we could give to You. Help us to be merciful as You are merciful.

THE MERCIFUL SAMARITAN

Do you think our culture is merciful? Why or why not?

Do you see yourself as merciful? Why or why not?

We live in the age of cancel culture, willing to cast people aside because of their failures and flaws. There's no room for grace and mercy on social media, where reactions are instant and everyone is expected to take a side. At the heart of our lack of mercy, however, is our inability to receive mercy. We're not merciful because we haven't experienced divine mercy. If you don't possess it, you cannot give it away.

Jesus once told a story about mercy from an unlikely source. Looking deeper into this story helps us see what it means to be merciful.

A QUESTION

Read Luke 10:25-29.

This well-known parable is actually an answer to trick question from a Jewish religious teacher.

What did the question in verse 29 reveal about the "expert in the law"?

How might someone ask this in the twenty-first century?

The expert's neighbor would have been another Jewish man. Like the expert in the law, we're tempted to limit our compassion and mercy to those like us. But Jesus corrected this assumption by telling a story about an unlikely neighbor who displayed mercy to an unlikely recipient.

AN ANSWER

Read Luke 10:30-37.

**Who would Jesus' audience have expected
to be the hero in this story?**

**What is Jesus trying to teach us by using a
Samaritan as an instrument of mercy?**

Jesus' original audience would have expected the priest or Levite to stop and attend to the injured man. Using a Samaritan would've been a shocking twist. Ethnically, Jews considered Samaritans unclean Gentiles because they were a mixture of Jewish and Gentile (pagan) blood. Samaritans didn't think too highly of the Jews either. Culturally, they saw life from vastly different perspectives. But this Samaritan became the hands and feet of God's mercy to an ailing man.

How did the Samaritan go out of his way to care for this man?

What can we learn from the Samaritan's act of mercy?

What does it look like for you to "Go and do the same" (v. 37)?

~~~~~~

LOOK AT YOURSELF

The neighbor who demands our mercy might not be the neighbor we wished for. Maybe it's someone with opposing political views or a different skin color; maybe it's a refugee family seeking safety in our country. The story of the good Samaritan shows us: Everyone is our neighbor, and everyone deserves mercy.

Who is your neighbor?

How can you show them mercy?

Prayer

Jesus, please help us embrace Your heart towards those in need. Help us remember that when we were lost and in need, You came to us in our distress. Grant us the heart to see our neighbors the way You do.

GO AND DO
THE SAME

This week we've pressed into the idea that mercy is more than a theological concept to grasp mentally. When mercy grips our hearts, it transforms our lives. In this personal study, we're going to look at three key truths about mercy that push towards action.

MERCY TOUCHES HUMAN SUFFERING

On the cross, Jesus took the sins of the world upon Himself. The King of heaven became a man of sorrows acquainted with human suffering and sin, so through His suffering we can become children of God. Because Jesus entered into our suffering, we follow the call to enter into the suffering and pain of others.

What's difficult or uncomfortable about engaging with other people's suffering?

If Jesus was willing to forsake His comfort for us, why do we resist forsaking our own comfort for others?

What human needs exist in your community? How can you meet these needs for the glory of Jesus?

MERCY CROSSES ETHNIC, CULTURAL, AND RELIGIOUS BARRIERS

Through the power of the cross, Jesus made a new ethnic group of people, comprised of people from all nations, called the Church.

Read Ephesians 2:13-16 and 1 Peter 2:9.

**What do these verses teach us about
the make up of God's people?**

**What boundaries keep you from ministering to people?
What would it take to cross those boundaries?**

**Where might God be calling you to cross
a boundary and meet a need?**

**Would you block out some time over the next week to pray
and ask God where you need to grow in this area? If so, when?**

MERCY COSTS US SOMETHING

Loving people doesn't require that we accept everything they do. It simply requires that we see people as God sees them—loved, valuable, and redeemable—and then treat them that way. No one comes to faith because a follower of Jesus was a mean-spirited jerk. God's kindness leads people to His kingdom (Rom. 2:4).

**What do you need to change in your life so
you can help more people in need?**

How can you use your time and talents to extend mercy?

What's one small act of mercy you can pursue this week?

Of the three points today, which is most challenging and why?

Prayer

Holy Spirit, please help us to care about being merciful as You are merciful, knowing that mercy reflects Your heart and leads us into Your happiness.

Week 6
the good life

HAPPY ARE THE
God-Seers

Start
WELCOME TO SESSION 6

What needs did you notice in your community over the last week? Did you respond? If not, when will you?

Last week, we talked about how the mercy of God leads us to become merciful—and happy—people. This week we're going to see how the good life comes to us as we set our eyes on God.

What's one thing you love about God?

In this session, we will learn what it means to be pure in the eyes of God. Once we become pure in Jesus, He invites us into life as a God-Seer. Happy are the pure because they will see God.

Watch

Use this space to take notes during the video teaching.

Discuss

Read Jesus' words together.

Blessed are the pure in heart,
for they will see God.
MATTHEW 5:8

Pastor Derwin said, "Those we admire we see higher."
What does it mean to have a high view of God? Why
is it important to have a high view of God?

God's holiness means He's completely pure and separate from
sin. Why is it necessary for us to understand this about God?

Read 1 John 1:7. How does Jesus' power to
cleanse our sin allow us to see God clearly?

What does it do for your faith to know Jesus
made us pure enough to see God?

How has seeing God through Jesus transformed your life?
How can you be a conduit of transformative grace for others?

Do you ever find it difficult to embrace the truth that
Jesus has made you clean and pure? If so, why?

OVER THE NEXT WEEK
Marinate on This

The higher we view God, the more we'll praise and
obey Him because of who He is and what He has
accomplished for us, not what we think he can give us.

Jesus is all that we could never be.

It's hard to be happy if you have a low opinion of yourself.
As we come to embrace that we by faith are all of who
Jesus is, then we'll begin to see ourselves as God sees us.

The greater we see Jesus, the more He'll influence
us because we're only capable of worshiping
someone whom we deem greater than us.

Grace empowers us to grow in holiness.

Jesus nailed our shame and guilt to the cross and cast
our sin into the sea of His forgotten memory.

God delights in giving us mercy and compassion.

Blessed are

THE PURE IN HEART,

for they will see God.

MATTHEW 5:8

ABSOLUTE PURITY

On the side of a hill overlooking the Sea of Galilee, Jesus continued His teaching on happiness.

Blessed are the pure in heart,
for they will see God.
MATTHEW 5:8

What comes to mind when you think about purity? Does this word have good or bad connotations? Why?

Out of all the Beatitudes, "Blessed are the pure in heart" may be the most difficult for our culture to engage. People either don't concern themselves with being pure, or they don't understand what it means. Jesus' original audience didn't have that problem.

To a Jewish person, purity extended far beyond sexual purity. In this Beatitude, Jesus was referring to the kind of purity God possesses. Jesus' audience knew the only way to see God was in the temple, in the Shekinah glory in the Holy of Holies. Only the high priest could enter once a year. To see the purest vision of God, the priest had to be the purest version of himself. He would be required to have perfect ritual purity and cleanliness.

Jesus' original audience would have known no one can see God and live (Ex. 33:20), but that's where God stepped in. The eternal Son of God clothed Himself in humanity, so we could see Him. Writing about His friend Jesus, the apostle John said:

We observed his glory, the glory as the one and only
Son from the Father, full of grace and truth.
JOHN 1:14

Through Jesus we see an exact representation of all God is (Heb. 1:3). Jesus, the Messiah, came as the bearer of the New Covenant. He wants to go beyond external purity and cleanliness to something deeper.

A DEEPER KIND OF PURITY

Read Jeremiah 31:33.

How does our relationship with Jesus change our relationship with God the Father?

Read 1 John 1:9.

How does Jesus make us pure?

The eternal Son of God came to stand in our stead at every single level of our existence. Because we're impure, He came to be our purity. He purifies our hearts and connects our new hearts to His Father's heart. All that He is, we are. By the Holy Spirit, when we believe in Christ for salvation, we're grafted into Him; because we're in Christ, what's true of Him becomes true of us. He became like us, so we can become like Him. When this happens we're able to see God for who He is. This is the good life.

How does proximity to Jesus make us pure?

SEE GOD; SEE YOURSELF

Being joined with Christ changes who we are from the inside out. The author of Hebrews described the change Jesus makes like this:

For by one offering he has perfected forever those who are sanctified.
HEBREWS 10:14

Underline the word that describes what Jesus has done for us.

How should we see ourselves now that we're joined with Christ?

**List three words you would use to describe
yourself. How would Jesus describe you?**

All that we could never be or measure up to, Jesus is for us. As our representative, Jesus is our "enough," our "measuring up." Jesus, the second person of the Trinity, is everything we need to have the good life. Through Jesus we've been made perfect, but that's not the way we see ourselves most of the time. If God has made us pure and perfect, what keeps us from feeling that way?

**Think back to your definition of purity on the
previous page. Now that you know Jesus' idea
of purity, how would you describe it now?**

Often our lack of happiness is interwoven with the lack of happiness we have in ourselves. Maybe someone did something awful to you, or you did something bad to someone else. Maybe you just feel unworthy, unknown, or unloved. Perhaps you feel like you'll never measure up. It's hard to be happy if you think you're bad.

As we come to embrace that all of who Jesus is, is all of who we are, we will begin to see ourselves the way God sees us—as beloved children. Our union in Christ is our reunion as the Father's beloved children.

Read Galatians 4:4-7.

What does it mean to be an heir?

What does it mean to be God's heir?
What rights does this give us?

When we come to see God by the Spirit through faith in Jesus, we're God's children. Your translation of the Scriptures may say "sons," but that's because in the ancient world property passed from fathers to sons. Paul is saying what belongs to Jesus is ours. All God's children see God as their *Abba,* or their dad. Jesus' sacred status is our sacred status. Our lives are forever grafted into His, so that God the Father sees us as He sees Jesus. This is grace.

Have you ever thought someone didn't deserve grace?
How is this different from the way God sees them?

End your study today by meditating on transforming grace.

*For if we have been united with him in the likeness of his death,
we will certainly also be in the likeness of his resurrection.*
ROMANS 6:5

**What difference does it make knowing Jesus
has raised you from death to life?**

*I have been crucified with Christ, and I no longer live, but
Christ lives in me. The life I now live in the body, I live by faith
in the Son of God, who loved me and gave himself for me.*
GALATIANS 2:20

**How does it change the way you see yourself to know the
Holy Spirit dwells inside of you at this very moment?**

See what great love the Father has given us that we should be called God's children—and we are!
1 JOHN 3:1

How does it make you feel to know you're a beloved child of a perfect Father?

Therefore, if anyone is in Christ, he is a new creation; the old has passed away, and see, the new has come!
2 CORINTHIANS 5:17

What difference does it make that the Holy Spirit has transformed you into a new creation?

Prayer

Jesus, thank You for making us pure and allowing us to see God. Thank You for changing us from the inside out. We're new, free, and pure because of Your grace.

WHAT GRACE DOES

In this week's video session, I shared the story of a woman caught in adultery who was brought to Jesus in the temple complex. From this encounter we see how God addressed our sin and replaced it with purity.

Read John 7:53–8:11.

Have you ever felt shame about yourself?

How can God use our shame to bring us closer to Him?

Shame causes the deterioration of one's soul. Shame says, "I am what I did." Shame becomes an engine that recycles abuse. It tells you that you'll never be good enough. Just as thunder follows lightning, guilt always follows shame. Guilt says, "I deserve how I feel. I'm guilty."

These are common feelings, even for a Christian. But Jesus offers a purifying grace greater than any shame or guilt. From this encounter we learn four truths. We'll look at two today and two in the next study.

GOD GIVES US HIS BEST EVEN THOUGH WE GIVE HIM OUR WORST

While the woman was a sinner, so were all the men who brought her to Jesus. The way they treated the woman stands in contrast to the way Jesus treated her. Because they weren't pure in heart, they didn't see God, so they didn't reflect God's faithful love, compassion, and mercy to this woman.

Read Romans 5:10.

What did you give God? What has He given you in return?

What sin are you holding onto that you need to hand over to Jesus, so He'll receive and forgive you?

GRACE STOOPS DOWN TO PICK US UP

None of us can stand in the light of God's holiness—not the woman caught in adultery, not the oppressive religious leaders, not those who picked up stones to harm her, not you or me. But when we're on the ground, we can look to Jesus to pick us up and bring us to God. He didn't condemn this woman, and He doesn't condemn those who look to Him in faith.

Read Romans 3:23-24.

When was a time you felt Jesus pick you up?

How has He continued to pick you up since that day?

Prayer

Father, thank You for sending Jesus to give us His best and lift us up when we had nothing to offer Him. Allow us to remember all He has done for us.

CONFORMING GRACE

In the last personal study we saw how grace transforms us. Today we're going to see how grace transforms the way we relate to others.

Read John 7:53-8:11 again.

GRACE SHOWS US THAT NO ONE HAS THE RIGHT TO THROW STONES AT ANOTHER PERSON

Implicit bias is an important concept to help us understand how we interact with one another. Broadly, it means that all of us carry attitudes and stereotypes about others that emerge involuntarily—we often don't even realize how we're acting. Often, these biases have to do with race or social status. But when we understand the grace of God in Christ Jesus, the very notion of our moral superiority quickly melts. The more we understand God's grace, the more we'll remember we are simply products of God's grace. Grace is the great equalizer because every saint has a past and every sinner has a future.

When was a time you thought you were better than someone else? What does Jesus have to say about that?

What changes do you need to make in your life so you see that everyone is a child of God?

GRACE EMPOWERS US TO GROW IN LOVE

The more we understand grace, the more we see that grace keeps, nourishes, and sustains us. Then we want to help people when they are caught in the snare of sin. We want to become healers, not condemners.

Read Titus 2:11-14.

Does your life reflect the grace of God? How should grace change the way we live?

To whom is God leading you to extend grace this week?

The only reason we could ever see God is that He gave us pure and clean hearts. Because of His grace to us, we become more gracious and merciful, giving us greater glimpses of His beauty. Pure-hearted people are eager to do good to others.

The good life is looking into the face of Jesus and seeing God. May His beauty make us beautiful.

Prayer

Lord Jesus, thank You for providing me grace to be conformed into Your image. May I always reflect Your abundant grace and extend it to others.

Week 7
the good life

HAPPY ARE THE

Peacemakers

Start

WELCOME TO SESSION 7

**How did last week shape your understanding
of what it means to be pure in Christ?**

**Share a time when you reconciled with someone
after an argument. How did it make you feel
to be at peace with that person again?**

Last week we talked about our purity before God, which comes after God reconciled us to Himself through Jesus. As the gospel has granted us peace with God, we find the good life as we extend that to others. In this session, we will talk about the happiness that comes from being reconciled with other people.

Watch

Use this space to take notes during the video teaching.

Discuss

Read Jesus' words together.

*Blessed are the peacemakers,
for they will be called sons of God.*
MATTHEW 5:9

**Becoming peacemakers flows out of the Holy Spirit,
empowering us to live righteously and mercifully. How does
this challenge your definition of being a peacemaker?**

**What did Jesus do to make peace
between you and His Father?**

**How does the peace Jesus gives us
empower us to be peacemakers?**

**As children of God, peace is a part of who we are in Christ. In what
area of life do you need to embrace this part of your identity?**

**When you consider your interactions online, are you a
peacemaker? How might we pursue peace in our virtual lives?**

**What does it look like for you to pursue peace across
racial and ethnic boundaries? Why is this necessary?**

OVER THE NEXT WEEK
Marinate on This

Peace, love, and forgiveness seem like beautiful ideas until God calls us to be peaceful, loving, and forgiving toward those who aren't.

Forgiveness of sins is the pathway to peace with God and with other image bearers.

The Beatitudes are a manifesto of hope that enable humanity to reimagine how beautiful and life-giving we could be under the rule and reign of King Jesus.

Becoming a peacemaker comes from the overflow of being empowered by God the Holy Spirit to live a righteous and merciful life.

The good life, a life of happiness, is loving God, ourselves, and all of humanity.

The early church was able to transform the Roman world because the resurrected Messiah brought different ethnic groups and classes of people together in unity.

Blessed are

THE PEACEMAKERS,

for they will be called sons of God.

MATTHEW 5:9

THE CALL TO MAKE PEACE

As Jesus continued his prescription for happiness, He said,

Blessed are the peacemakers,
for they will be called sons of God.
MATTHEW 5:9

Reread Matthew 5:7-9. How are these three Beatitudes related?

Pursuing peace (Matt. 5:9) is intertwined with hungering and thirsting for righteousness and being merciful (Matt. 5:7-8). Becoming a peacemaker requires that God has first brought us into peace with Him through the forgiveness that comes by grace through faith in Jesus. Then out of the overflow of the Holy Spirit's power, God enables us to live righteously and mercifully in response to the gospel.

Read Romans 5:1.

What did God do to pursue peace with us?

Notice that Jesus said happy are the peacemakers, not happy are the peaceful. What's the difference?

God's righteousness has always been about embodying God's love, and God's love is always merciful. The good life—a life of happiness—is loving God, ourselves, and all of humanity. In the kingdom of God, there's "righteousness, peace, and joy in the Holy Spirit" (Rom. 14:17). Peace isn't passive. Being peaceful is a fleeting state of mind. Peacemaking is an active, God-given pursuit. It's the intentional act of God in Christ reconciling us to Himself through the cross and enabling us to extend peace to others. Making peace is hard, happy gospel work.

Does it surprise you to hear that peacemaking is "work"? Why must peace be actively sought instead of passively assumed?

FIRST-CENTURY EXPECTATIONS

The world Jesus lived in was chaotic, violent, and tumultuous. Jewish men were awaiting the Messiah to usher in peace by eradicating the Romans from their homeland, and the Romans believed Caesar would usher in peace. Rome's method of ensuring peace was through force and brutality.

How was Jesus' peace different from the peace the world expected?

Jesus saw and experienced Roman oppression, the hardships of being poor, and life on the margins of society. Jesus' peace extended beyond the borders of circumstance. It didn't fit others' expectations. People could only experience the peace Jesus taught about through communion with God. When we say the happiness He taught about was more than the good feeling you get when something nice happens to you, we know Jesus meant it. He experienced it constantly.

MAKING PEACE WHEN IT'S HARD

Read Romans 12:19-21.

**When was a time you acted as a peacemaker?
What was hard about it?**

**What keeps you from experiencing peace
and making peace with others?**

**Is there anyone you're holding a grudge against? How might
letting that go lead to a greater sense of happiness?**

When Jesus correlated our happiness with being peacemakers in a world of violence, injustice, and hardship, people would have seen that as radical. Jesus' method of eradicating the Romans from the promised land wasn't to cast them out with the sword, but to usher them into the peace of God, so they could become peaceful people. For Jesus, seeking vengeance is a tool of the ungodly. The Prince of peace entered a world devoid of peace to create peacemakers.

Prayer

Holy Spirit, help us to be people of peace in a world that needs the peace You secured with Your blood on the cross.

IT'S IN THE DNA

Just as children resemble their parents, all of God's children resemble Him. Those of us united with Christ have been adopted into God's family, and peacemaking is a family trait. The term "sons of God" is a Hebrew idiom for family resemblance. The Holy Spirit's primary task is to conform us to the image of Christ Jesus (Rom. 8:29). Along those lines, let's do a self-diagnostic.

**Would people who know you best say you're
a peacemaker? Why or why not?**

**Would people who read your social media posts
say you're a peacemaker? Why or why not?**

**Would people who know you say you participate in
gossip, slander, deception, and lies? Explain.**

How would people who know you say you handle conflict?

How would people say you interact with others whose beliefs are different than yours?

Would people say you pursue peace amid the racial and political divisions in America? Why or why not?

The more we soak in God's peace through Christ, the more forgiving, merciful, kind, and compassionate we'll become, because He'll soften our hard hearts with His grace. His love draws us deeper into His heart, and we start resembling Him as we follow Him by faith. Thus, the God of peace will express His peace through us.

Being transformed into the image of Jesus isn't automatic. Just as we entered God's kingdom through faith, we also grow as God's children by faith. It's often slower and more painful than we would like, but by God's grace, we cooperate with Him in the process of becoming more like Jesus.

Based on this diagnostic, where do you need to grow?

What are three things you can do this week to be a peacemaker?

What can you do specifically on social media to be a peacemaker?

Prayer

God, use these questions to convict us to live according to Your purposes in our lives. As You've made peace with us, help us to pursue peace with others.

ETHNIC PEACEMAKING

When we believe the gospel, we become peacemakers because God is a peacemaker. Our peace with God should cause us to seek peace with all people. The living and active grace of God created a new race of people. This new humanity is called the Church. Together, we're one in the gospel. Today we're going to consider what it might look like for us to pursue peace with brothers and sisters who may not look like us.

GOD GETTING HIS FAMILY BACK

Read Galatians 3:8.

Through the life, death, and resurrection of Jesus, not only are we forgiven, made righteous, regenerated, and indwelt with the Spirit, but we're also adopted into God's united, transcultural family. As God's family, we're not color-blind; we're color-blessed. We're a diverse and beautiful community of siblings.

Why is it important to understand that God's plan includes a transcultural family?

How does this change the way you relate to brothers and sisters in Christ from different ethnicities than you?

A FAMILY OF ONENESS

Read Galatians 3:27-29.

If we belong to Christ, we're clothed in Christ's righteousness, and we're heirs of the promise that God fulfilled in Christ Jesus. It's hard to look down on someone who is clothed in Christ, just like you. Our ethnic, class, and gender differences are transformed, so that they're no longer points of division, but celebration. In the gospel, our differences become tools of grace to grow us.

Why does America still struggle with major racial divides? What about your own state or community?

PEACE AND RECONCILIATION BETWEEN ETHNIC GROUPS

Read Ephesians 2:14-16.

As Jesus' multicolored family, our peace with God and each other is secured by Him. Grace indeed creates a new ethnicity of "differents."

Do you live as though there is still a "dividing wall of hostility" (v. 14)? What does it look like to embrace the broken wall?

NEW RELATIONSHIPS ACROSS ETHNIC GROUPS

Read Colossians 3:13.

Out of love for our siblings, we cultivate a posture of listening and learning, seeking to understand before being understood. This requires us to obey Paul's words.

What steps could you take to live a more diverse life? Whom could you spend time with?

Think back to the idea of implicit bias. What implicit biases might you have? What can you do to address them?

A DIVERSE CHURCH

Read Revelation 5:8-10.

We need to catch a vision for God's heart concerning the church on earth, and how it can look like the church in the new heavens and new earth. One day, all nations will worship together at the throne of God (v. 9). In that day, our differences will be celebrated alongside our unity in Christ. We should want our churches on earth to look like worship in heaven.

Is your church diverse? Why is that important?

Spend a few moments praying for the leaders in your church. Ask God to lead them toward a God-glorifying vision of diversity.

TAKEAWAYS

What's the most significant truth you've learned from today's study?

What's your biggest opportunity for growth?

As we engage in peacemaking and building bridges of ethnic reconciliation in the church and outside the church, we'll be called children of God (Matt. 5:9). Wouldn't it be nice for us as followers of Jesus to be known for making peace? This is the good life.

Prayer

Father, please help our churches and our lives to be as diverse as the new heavens and new earth will be. Lord, we long to have peace among our brothers and sisters of different backgrounds. We pray that Your peacemaking gospel would bring peace to all our relationships.

Week 8

the good life

HAPPY ARE THE
Persecuted

WELCOME TO SESSION 8

How did last week's session challenge or enhance your understanding of what it means to make peace?

As we end our time together we'll consider the last Beatitude, happy are the persecuted.

How would you say our culture feels about the church? Why do you think they feel this way?

In this last session, we will learn that happy are those who are persecuted for their identification with Jesus. While it may be unsettling to think of persecution bringing happiness, God often reveals His redemptive plan through persecution.

Use this space to take notes during the video teaching.

Discuss

Read Jesus' words together.

*Blessed are those who are persecuted because of righteousness,
for the kingdom of heaven is theirs.
You are blessed when they insult you and persecute you and
falsely say every kind of evil against you because of me. Be glad
and rejoice, because your reward is great in heaven. For that
is how they persecuted the prophets who were before you.*
MATTHEW 5:10-12

**What does it mean to be persecuted "because of righteousness"?
How is this different than what we may think of as persecution?**

**Have you ever experienced any kind of backlash
because of your faith? How did you respond?**

**What was Jesus' posture toward persecution? What does
it look like to respond to mistreatment like Jesus?**

**How was God's redemptive plan
fulfilled through persecution?**

**What should our posture be as the church is
pushed even more toward the margin? How can we
point to Jesus even in a changing culture?**

**Praying for those who persecute us fortifies
our hearts and makes us like Christ. How can
you love and pray for others today?**

OVER THE NEXT WEEK
Marinate on This

In Christ, we're a resilient and remarkable people
because our God is resilient and remarkable.

Our post-Christian culture is a fertile environment
for the church in America to experience revival.

In God's sovereign goodness, He'll take persecution
and use it to teach us how to rely on Him to provide.

Life in the margins requires a deeper level of understanding
of the beauty of our faith, a higher commitment to be the
Church in the world, and a stronger cultivation of discipleship.

The holy fire of revival will be one of prayer, ethnic
reconciliation, mercy, mission, and holistic discipleship.

Blessed are

THOSE WHO ARE PERSECUTED BECAUSE OF RIGHTEOUSNESS,

for the kingdom of heaven is theirs.

You are blessed when they insult you and persecute you and falsely say every kind of evil against you because of me.

Be glad and rejoice, because your reward is great in heaven. For that is how they persecuted the prophets who were before you.

MATTHEW 5:10-12

HAPPINESS IN HARDSHIP

Jesus' last Beatitude says,

> *Blessed are those who are persecuted because of righteousness,*
> *for the kingdom of heaven is theirs.*
> *You are blessed when they insult you and persecute you and*
> *falsely say every kind of evil against you because of me. Be glad*
> *and rejoice, because your reward is great in heaven. For that is*
> *how they persecuted the prophets who were before you."*
> MATTHEW 5:10-12

Does it make you nervous to know that life with
Jesus will be fraught with trials and persecution?
How does the Lord bring us comfort?

The fires of persecution have a way of burning off the impurities, so Jesus can form His character in us. But the Beatitude we're studying this week can be difficult to take in and absorb. Persecution and suffering? These are not fun, nor will they ever be. We have to trust Jesus when we don't understand. Where else can we go? No one else has the words of eternal life but Him (John 6:68).

As we decide by faith to pursue the good life and experience the kingdom of God, we'll encounter persecution and opposition from the dark powers that rule this present age. At the very least, we'll experience internal spiritual persecution as we fight sin and shed the old way of living. In those moments we can either turn to Jesus or worldly tactics to fight against persecution.

Christianity has been increasingly pushed to the margins of American life. How can we use that as an opportunity?

What worldly comforts do you often turn to instead of Jesus?

When we pursue God's righteousness and His kingdom, we'll experience backlash. We'll be mocked and disliked by friends, coworkers, and neighbors. When we choose sexual purity as an act of worship, others will make fun of us and dislike us. When we choose forgiveness over bitterness and love over hate, people will call us soft. When we choose Jesus over political parties, the world will reject us. But all of this is beneficial for us. Rejection puts us in a position of weakness where we have to depend on Jesus alone.

POWER IN WEAKNESS

Read 2 Corinthians 12:9-10.

What does it mean to "take pleasure" in weakness (v. 10)?

Taking pleasure means to be happy. God calls us to be happy when He reveals our weaknesses, when others insult us, and when we experience hardships, persecutions, and difficulties for Christ's sake. In these moments, we rely on the power of Christ residing in us. We're at our strongest when we're at our weakest.

**When have you felt the unique presence
and power of Jesus in hardship?**

Read John 15:20.

How is persecution evidence that we're truly following Jesus?

If we follow Jesus, we'll see persecution. This doesn't mean we should seek persecution, but rather if we're living righteous lives, we should expect persecution. Jesus was persecuted. The apostles were persecuted. The early church was persecuted, and we will be also. But Jesus makes an astonishing promise: when we're insulted, falsely accused, and persecuted, we should be glad and rejoice. Why? Because we have an epic reward (Matt. 5:12)—the triune God Himself. Eternal happiness becomes ours. The early church understood this well. Looking at their experience can lend understanding to ours.

PERSECUTION AND THE SPREAD OF THE GOSPEL

*But you will receive power when the Holy Spirit has come
on you, and you will be my witnesses in Jerusalem, in
all Judea and Samaria, and to the end of the earth.*

ACTS 1:8

In Acts 1:8, Jesus restated the Great Commission (Matt. 28:18-20) and sent His disciples out into the world to spread His glory and name to all the nations. This verse in Acts provides the geographical outline of Acts: Jerusalem, chapters 1–7; Judea and Samaria, chapters 8–12; ends of the earth (i.e., Rome) in chapters 13–28. But the disciples had a difficult time beginning the task.

Read Acts 8:1-4.

What did God allow to happen to them in order that they would scatter?

Instead of going to the nations, the disciples stayed put. But starting in Acts 4, the disciples began to experience persecution that reached its culmination in chapter 8 when they were scattered from Jerusalem and sent on their way. God used persecution to drive them forward on their mission.

Read Acts 11:19-24.

What diversity do you see in these verses?

How was God's redemptive plan fulfilled through persecution?

The rest of the Book of Acts tells the story of this small band of disciples scattering all over the known world. Everywhere they went, the gospel transformed people. Within 300 years, this tiny fringe group overwhelmed the Roman Empire with the gospel.

PROMISES FOR PERSECUTION

Read Romans 8:31-39.

List all the promises of God you find in these verses.

**Why should these promises give us hope when
we face hardship and persecution?**

**According to Paul, how does hardship lead
us into the happiness of God?**

When we suffer as Jesus did, we become more like Him than we were before. Our lives look more like that of the happiest man who ever lived. When we suffer, Jesus is with us. That's why Paul was able to say that no created thing would ever be able to separate us from the love of God in Christ Jesus. Guess what? Everything but God is a created thing! That means that nothing in all the world will ever separate us from Jesus. And His power, presence, peace, and purpose are with us during persecution, so we can be happy, knowing our reward is in heaven. This is the good life.

Prayer

Thank you, Jesus, for always being with us. Help us to endure well for the sake of Your name, so we can make Your happiness known to all the nations.

HOW DID JESUS HANDLE PERSECUTION?

Paul wrote to his young apprentice Timothy:

All who want to live a godly life in Christ Jesus will be persecuted.
2 TIMOTHY 3:12

If persecution is a matter of if, not when, we need to figure out how we'll respond before persecution comes to us. For that we need to look no further than the life of Jesus Christ. From His life and ministry, we can learn how to respond to persecution.

JESUS HAD CLARITY IN CHAOS

Think about all of Jesus' interactions in the Gospels. Can you recall a time when He lost control or clarity?

Think of a time you experienced something chaotic. Was it difficult to keep your cool? Why is it important to keep a clear head in chaos?

Jesus was slandered, mocked, and misrepresented through His earthly ministry. Jewish religious leaders followed Him constantly, seeking to discredit Him. Eventually He was beaten, tortured, and executed, but in all the chaos Jesus had clarity, because He knew who He was.

JESUS KNEW HIS IDENTITY

As the true human, Jesus lived in perfect communion and union with the Father by the Spirit's power. Through Jesus' death and resurrection, God has made us His children. The more we find ourselves in Christ, the more we can stand in truth and not be swayed by deception.

Read Matthew 3:17.

**What did Jesus know about Himself that
we forget about ourselves?**

Why do we forget so easily?

**What are some ways you could regularly remind
yourself of who you are in Christ?**

How might doing this make a noticeable difference?

When we find our identity in the deep love of God, we're secure enough not to allow the chaos to cloud our vision as we testify to the kingdom of God. Often in chaos and persecution, followers of Jesus lose their cool because they forget their identity and fall prey to deception. During chaos we can remain composed and loving in the face of those who oppose Christ in us. This is an act of worship that displays heaven on earth.

WE ROOT OURSELVES IN OUR IDENTITY

Human beings have an innate desire to preserve and defend themselves. When we forget that Jesus is our defense, we'll quickly lose our composure. In our toughest moments we need to remember we belong to Jesus and can draw from the well of His strength and endurance.

Read 1 Peter 2:22-23.

**How does remembering our identity
help us model Jesus' response?**

Read Matthew 5:44-45.

**How does praying for people change our hearts
toward them even when they mistreat us?**

Jesus endured persecution without lying, insulting, or sinning in return. He trusted God and loved His persecutors. He prayed for them even as they were killing Him. Through the Holy Spirit's power, we can do the same. And when we love our enemies and pray for those who persecute us, we're not only pointing them to the gospel of Christ, but we're also administering divine healing into our souls and spreading God's grace to others.

Prayer

Holy Spirit, help us to depend upon You for endurance, security, and identity as we face persecution.

LIFE ON THE MARGINS

In this session, hopefully you've seen that persecution can and does lead to happiness and God's redemptive purpose flourishing in the world. Life on the margins helps us understand the beauty of our faith on a deeper level and strengthens our commitment to disciple fellow believers and be the church in the world.

Imagine what it would be like to be so lost in God's love that we can't even be offended. This is the good life: when our joy isn't found in external circumstances, but in the eternal God of love. This is the purest form of happiness. The magnificence of our triune God's beauty captures our gaze. No wonder the Psalmist said,

Those who look to him are radiant with joy;
their faces will never be ashamed.
PSALM 34:5

Would your unchurched friends say you resemble the person in the verse above? Why or why not?

When was the last time you invited someone to church?

Do you think the church will remain a priority for you as you become an adult? Why or why not?

Persecution can't steal our joy because our joy never came from our circumstances in the first place. We are looking at God, not our surroundings. He even takes the ups and downs of life and reshapes them into a blessing that makes us more like who we were meant to be. Even when we lose, we win. Why? Because in God's kingdom there is no losing—only lessons that teach and equip us. Because our joy is constant, it can always be spread.

Read 1 Peter 2:12.

As the world marginalizes us, why should we continue to seek and pursue righteousness?

How can you help your church be so vital and valued in your community that they would miss it if it ceased to exist?

Do you know people who are suspicious or hostile toward Christianity? How could you serve and love them this week?

Prayer

God, please help us to find a joy so deep that persecution and marginalization can't shake it. May You keep and maintain our joy regardless of our circumstances. Teach us to be people who place their hope in You alone.

A Happiness Manifesto

Congrats! You've made it to the end of the study. The Sermon on the Mount is Jesus' manifesto on what it looks like to live the good life. Jesus' teaching provides a pathway to a life governed by fullness and happiness. In the spirit of Jesus' teaching, here's what we're calling A Happiness Manifesto.

Read over it, commit to it, and go forward in the happiness to which Jesus has called you.

the good life

I, _____ ,

declare that all I would ever hope to be is found in all of who Jesus is. My life is hidden in His life. His life is my life.

As a gift of grace, Jesus lived a sinless life because I couldn't.

In His unending mercy, Jesus died the death I should have died to atone for my sins. Today, I'm free from the power of sin and death.

Because of His great love for me, I'm a holy, blameless, righteous, adopted child of God. I am pleasing to the Father because I'm His beloved child.

The happiness I seek can never be satisfied by created things.

The happiness I was created to experience is not found in my circumstances.

True happiness is more about God making me good than good things happening to me.

Today, I declare that I choose happiness because I choose Jesus, His kingdom, and His glory.

Today, I declare that I will choose the ways of His kingdom, the truth of His gospel, and live from His life.

Signed _____ Date _____

TIPS FOR LEADING A SMALL GROUP

Prayerfully Prepare

Prepare for each group session with prayer. Ask the Holy Spirit to work through you and the group discussion as you point to Jesus each week through God's Word.

REVIEW the personal studies and the group sessions ahead of time.

PRAY for each person in the group.

Minimize Distractions

Do everything in your ability to help people focus on what's most important: connecting with God, the Bible, and one another.

Create a comfortable environment. If group members are uncomfortable, they'll be distracted and therefore not engaged in the group experience.

Take into consideration seating, temperature, lighting, refreshments, surrounding noise, and general cleanliness.

At best, thoughtfulness and hospitality show guests and group members they're welcome and valued in whatever environment you choose to gather. At worst, people may never notice your effort, but they're also not distracted.

Include Others

Your goal is to foster a community that welcomes people just as they are but also encourages them to grow spiritually. Always be aware of opportunities to include anyone who visits the group and invite new people to join.

Encourage Discussion

A good small group experience has the following characteristics:

EVERYONE PARTICIPATES. Encourage students to ask questions, share responses, or read aloud.

NO ONE DOMINATES—NOT EVEN THE LEADER. Be sure your time speaking as a leader takes up less than half your time together as a group. Politely guide the discussion if anyone dominates.

NOBODY IS RUSHED THROUGH QUESTIONS. Don't feel that a moment of silence is a bad thing. People often need time to think about their responses to questions they've just heard or to gain courage to share what God is stirring in their hearts.

INPUT IS AFFIRMED AND FOLLOWED UP. Make sure you point out something true or helpful in a response. Don't just move on. Build community with follow-up questions, asking how other students have experienced similar things or how a truth has shaped their understanding of God and the Scripture you're studying. Students are less likely to speak up if they fear that you don't actually want to hear their answers or that you're only looking for certain answers.

GOD AND HIS WORD ARE CENTRAL. Opinions and experiences can be helpful, but God has given us the truth. Trust Scripture to be the authority and God's Spirit to work in students' lives. You can't change anyone, but God can. Continually point students to the Word and to active steps of faith.

Keep Connecting

Think of ways to connect with students during the week. Participation always improves when members spend time connecting with one another outside the group sessions. The more people are comfortable with and involved in one another's lives, the more they'll look forward to being together. When people move beyond being friendly to truly being friends who form a community, they come to each session eager to engage instead of merely attending.

Session 1

START

Welcome students. Start with a quick activity: Go around the group and have everyone say their name and one thing that makes them happy that starts with the same letter. Go first, and make sure to explain your answer.

Use the group questions on the top of p. 10 to transition into the lesson.

Ask someone to pray, then watch the video teaching.

WATCH

Play the video for Session 1. Take notes as students watch the video and be prepared to follow up with specific questions they may have.

DISCUSS

After watching, use your notes to highlight a few points from the video. Invite a volunteer to read something from their notes that stuck out to them. Then use the questions on p. 11 to lead students in group discussion.

Before you go, point students to the "Marinate on This" statements on p. 12. Challenge them to pick one statement and post to Instagram this week. (Make sure you follow them so you can hold them accountable!)

Close in prayer and remind students to complete the three personal studies before the next group meeting.

Session 2

START

Start with a quick game of friendly debate. Pose a few simple questions to the room: Which is better, pizza or tacos? Movies or video games? LeBron or MJ? Have everyone divide into sides of the room and choose a spokesperson to defend their answer.

Bring everyone back together and review any questions from the previous week. Use the group questions on the top of p. 26 to transition into the lesson.

Ask someone to pray, then watch the video teaching.

WATCH

Play the video for Session 2. Take notes as students watch the video and be prepared to follow up with specific questions they may have.

DISCUSS

After watching, use your notes to highlight a few points from the video. Invite a volunteer to read something from their notes that stuck out to them.

Then use the questions on p. 27 to lead students in group discussion.

When you're done, look ahead to the "Marinate on This" statements. Bring some index cards and pens and have students write down one statement that sticks out to them. Tell them to put it in a visible place this week where they'll see it every day.

Close in prayer and remind students to complete the three personal studies before the next group meeting.

Session 3

START
Bring a foam ball and explain that it's the "share an interesting fact" ball. Say something interesting about yourself. Toss it to someone else and have them play until it goes around the room.

Bring everyone back together and review any questions from the previous week. Use the group questions on the top of p. 42 to transition into the lesson.

Ask someone to pray, then watch the video teaching.

WATCH
Play the video for Session 3. Take notes as students watch the video and be prepared to follow up with specific questions they may have.

DISCUSS
After watching, use your notes to highlight a few points from the video. Invite a volunteer to read something from their notes that stuck out to them. Then use the questions on p. 43 to lead students in group discussion.

Look over the "Marinate on This" statements on p. 44. Instruct students to read a statement each day and circle a word or two that sticks out to them. Use the margins or the space at the bottom to jot down notes. (Tell them you're going to follow up next week—and make sure you do!)

Close in prayer and remind students to complete the three personal studies before the next group meeting.

Session 4

START
Start with a quick activity. Bring enough paper and pens for everyone and have students draw a flag containing some objects that symbolize who they are. Show your own—maybe it's a guitar, tennis racket, a book, or a cup of coffee. Invite volunteers to share their flags and the meaning of what they drew.

Bring everyone back together and review any questions from the previous week. Use the group questions on the top of p. 58 to transition into the lesson.

Ask someone to pray, then watch the video teaching.

WATCH

Play the video for Session 4. Take notes as students watch the video and be prepared to follow up with specific questions they may have.

DISCUSS

After watching, use your notes to highlight a few points from the video. Invite a volunteer to read something from their notes that stuck out to them. Then use the questions on p. 59 to lead students in group discussion.

Throughout the week, text each person in the group one of the "Marinate on This" statements on p. 60. Make sure you use their name and let them know you're praying for them.

Close in prayer and remind students to complete the three personal studies before the next group meeting.

Session 5

START

Start with an activity. Divide the group into groups of three. Each group has to find something they all have in common—the weirder the better. After a few minutes, invite everyone to share, then vote on which group wins.

Bring everyone back together and review any questions from the previous week. Use the group questions on the top of p. 74 to transition into the lesson.

Ask someone to pray, then watch the video teaching.

WATCH

Play the video for Session 5. Take notes as students watch the video and be prepared to follow up with specific questions they may have.

DISCUSS

After watching, use your notes to highlight a few points from the video. Invite a volunteer to read something from their notes that stuck out to them. Then use the questions on p. 75 to lead students in group discussion.

There are seven "Marinate on This" statements on p. 76. Direct students to write out one statement each day this week, giving thanks to God for His mercy in their lives.

Close in prayer and remind students to complete the three personal studies before the next group meeting.

Session 6

START

Start with a game of Desert Island. Ask each student to name one thing they would bring if they were stranded on a desert island. When you're done, divide the room into small groups and tell them to combine their items in order to increase their chances for survival. Go around and share each group's crazy solution.

Bring everyone back together and review any questions from the previous week. Use the group questions on the top of p. 90 to transition into the lesson.

Ask someone to pray, then watch the video teaching.

WATCH

Play the video for Session 6. Take notes as students watch the video and be prepared to follow up with specific questions they may have.

DISCUSS

After watching, use your notes to highlight a few points from the video.

Invite a volunteer to read something from their notes that stuck out to them. Then use the questions on p. 91 to lead students in group discussion.

Point students to the "Marinate on This" statements on p. 92. Tell them to read a statement every day—how can they turn each one into a prayer that would help them see God higher?

Close in prayer and remind students to complete the three personal studies before the next group meeting.

Session 7

START

Start with a quick activity. Instead of Two Truths and a Lie, play Two Lies and a Truth—have each person come up with two false statements about themselves and one truth. As each person shares, vote as a group about which statement is true.

Bring everyone back together and review any questions from the previous week. Use the group questions on the top of p. 106 to transition into the lesson.

Ask someone to pray, then watch the video teaching.

WATCH

Play the video for Session 7. Take notes as students watch the video and be prepared to follow up with specific questions they may have.

DISCUSS

After watching, use your notes to highlight a few points from the video. Invite a volunteer to read something from their notes that stuck out to them. Then use the questions on p. 107 to lead students in group discussion.

Point students to the "Marinate on This" statements on p. 108. As they read them throughout the week, is there someone they need to make peace with? Have them thank God for His forgiveness, then forgive anyone who might need it—even if they don't seem to deserve it.

Close in prayer and remind students to complete the three personal studies before the next group meeting.

Session 8

START

Start with the "One Word" game. Divide students into small groups. Then, tell them to think back over all seven lessons and come up with one word that describes happiness. As they share, lead a discussion about how their idea

of happiness has changed since the first meeting.

Bring everyone back together and review any questions from the previous week. Use the group questions on the top of p. 122 to transition into the lesson.

Ask someone to pray, then watch the video teaching.

WATCH

Play the video for Session 8. Take notes as students watch the video and be prepared to follow up with specific questions they may have.

DISCUSS

After watching, use your notes to highlight a few points from the video. Invite a volunteer to read something from their notes that stuck out to them. Then use the questions on p. 123 to lead students in group discussion.

Look over the "Marinate on This" statements on p. 124. At the bottom, have students write down the names of three people they will pray for this week: One should be a leader in their church, one should be a family member, and one should be a friend or classmate.

Close in prayer, thanking God for your group and how He's working in their lives.